CONCORD PUBLIC LIBRARY
45 GREEN STREET
CONCORD, NH 03301

DISCARDED

Contents

Chapter One
The Birth of the Renaissance   4

Chapter Two
The Social Order   12

Chapter Three
Duties, Dangers, and Delights   22

Chapter Four
Artists and Patrons, Thinkers and Doers   32

Notes   42

Glossary   44

For Further Exploration   45

Index   47

The Birth of the Renaissance

Florence is often called the birthplace of the Italian Renaissance. This is a good description, because a renaissance is a new beginning. This rebirth of learning and art began in Florence in the 1300s and lasted for about two hundred years. As its ideas spread to other parts of Italy, Florence became the model for other Italian cities.

The City-States of Italy

Italy was not a united country at the time of the Renaissance. Instead, it was made up of separate city-states. There were over two hundred of them. Some of them—such as Florence, Venice, and Milan—were large, sometimes with as many as one hundred thousand people. Others were much smaller, with populations that were never more than five thousand to ten thousand.

These cities shared some history and traditions, but they were otherwise independent of each other. They had separate governments and separate customs. Even the languages they spoke were really different **dialects** of what

The Birth of the Renaissance

had been one language, the Latin of the ancient Romans. As a result, a man traveling to another city might not be able to understand the dialect used there nor make himself understood.

Though Italy was part of the Holy Roman Empire, the emperors were far away in Germany. They could not control the cities. Not even the popes in Rome had enough power to control them. This left the cities free to develop their own forms of political and cultural life.

From Rome to the Renaissance

The ancient Romans had studied many of the ideas of ancient Greece. They spread this Greco-Roman civilization throughout Italy and much of Europe. However, the

Ruins of ancient Roman structures, like the Colosseum in Rome, gave the city-states of Renaissance Italy a feeling of connection with their shared Roman past.

The Birth of the Renaissance

mighty Roman Empire finally collapsed. Then Italy had to **endure** hundreds of years of control by the foreign countries that invaded its lands.

In the 1300s, the Roman Empire had long since disappeared from Italy. Yet there were reminders of its lost culture everywhere. Some were in the form of ruins, all that was left of the great monuments and buildings the Romans had erected. Still, these ruins were enough to give Florentines, as the people of Florence are called, a sense of connection with the ancient past. Benvenuto Cellini, a great Florentine sculptor and goldsmith, describes some of these sites in his autobiography: "It is written in the [records] of our Florentine ancestors . . . that the city of Florence was [clearly] built in imitation of the fair city of Rome, and [the parts that remain] of the Colosseum and Baths can still be seen."[1]

Rediscovered Treasures

Still other traces of the past were the writings of the great thinkers of that early civilization. Since they were written in Greek or Latin, though, few people could actually read or understand them. However, as more and more of these treasures were rediscovered, educated Florentines eagerly began to learn Greek and Latin so that they could read the original texts.

It was the discovery and translation of these great works that set the Italian Renaissance into motion. Florentines felt that by studying the lives of the great minds of the past they could learn how to deal with their own problems. In his *Book of the Family,* Leon Battista Alberti, a Florentine artist and student of the Greek and Latin classics, reminded his readers of "what ancient records and the [memories] of our elders... together can teach us."[2]

At first, collectors who wanted to have a copy of some newly found treasure had to spend long hours making a copy of it by hand. They could also hire copyists to do the work for them. Then came the invention of the printing press in the fifteenth century. That meant there could be many more copies of each work made with much less effort. The books that came off the new printing presses helped to spread the knowledge and ideas of the Renaissance.

Why Florence?

There were several reasons why Florence was an ideal starting place for the Renaissance. One was its healthy economy. Florence lies in Tuscany, a fertile region with many farms. The soil in Tuscany is good for growing grain, grapes, and olives. In the city itself, the two most important businesses were textiles and banking. Florentines invented a process for improving the quality of wool. This process allowed merchants to import unfinished wool, turn it into the finest-quality textiles, and export it to other countries.

Florentine bankers were also very successful. They were known all through Europe. The wealth that the textile and banking industries brought to the city helped pay for the city's **thriving** cultural life.

The Treasures of Florence

Perhaps the greatest assets Florence had, though, were the talents of so many of its people. It is not surprising

With its healthy economy and the creative talent of its people, Florence was an ideal starting place for the Renaissance.

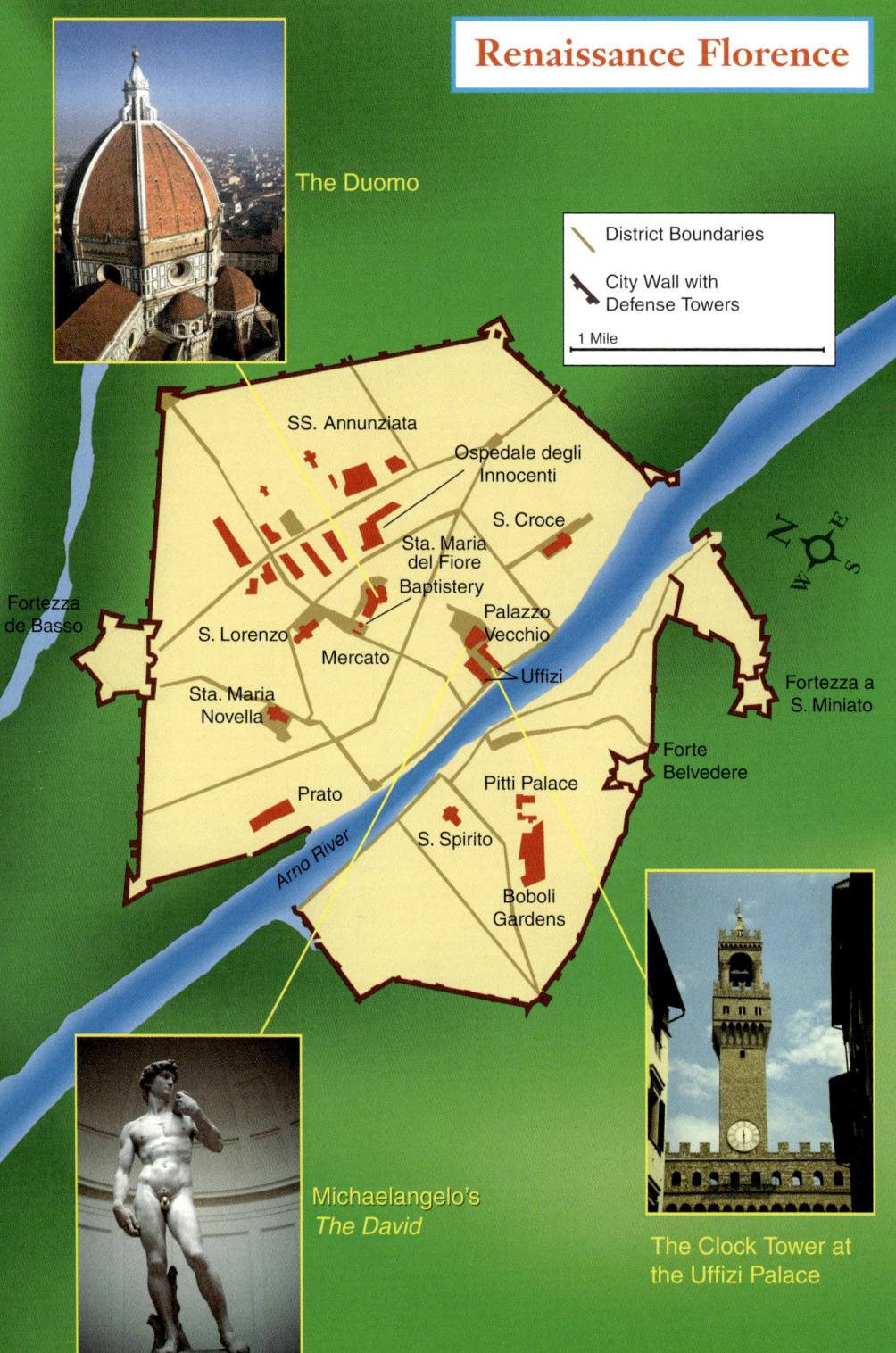

that Benvenuto Cellini thought of his home city as being inspired by ancient Rome. If anything, though, Florence's talented architects, sculptors, and painters tried to go beyond the glory of Rome. Their genius could be seen in the very look of the city. Broad public squares called piazzas were lined with grand palaces and churches. Inside these great buildings were sculptures and paintings by the most famous artists of the time. Literature also thrived in Florence. Schools passed this learning on to future generations, while libraries collected works of both the past and present.

The number of people involved in the most creative and **scholarly** work was actually just a small part of the population of Florence. Still, for every artist who worked in stone or marble, there was a small army of support, including builders, bricklayers, haulers to move materials, and other laborers. Then there were the bankers, lawyers, and clerks who did the paperwork—and found the money—for all this construction. In the same way, a labor force of spinners, dyers, weavers, haulers, and many others supported the textile merchants.

The flowering of the arts, **scholarship**, and wealth in Florence during the Renaissance was truly amazing. Perhaps it was only fitting for a city whose name comes from a Latin word for "blooming."

CHAPTER TWO

The Social Order

Society in Renaissance Italy was a mix of many different kinds of people. A person's place in that society depended on many things. Birth was one, but natural skills and talents were also important. Where someone lived counted, as did gender. Women had fewer chances for success than men did. Also, a woman's place in society could change, depending on whether she was single, married, or widowed.

Especially in the wealthier classes, people were judged by their appearance. Skin, hair, clothing, and jewelry all played a part in deciding how well someone fit into a group. Also, each social group expected certain kinds of behavior.

Country Life

The Italian countryside contained many farms. Sometimes the people who worked on the farms owned the land. However, much of that land was owned and controlled by landlords. Some of these landlords were of the richer, titled class. These nobles collected money for many

Wealthy nobles owned most of the farms in the Italian countryside. Peasants, however, did all of the backbreaking work on these farms.

activities connected with their land and the people who worked on it. This could include taxes, fines in court cases, and fees for hunting or fishing licenses.

The people who did the real work on the landlords' farms were the peasants. They were not paid for their work. Their income was based on selling what they raised. Out of that money, they had to pay rent for the land they used. If they did not pay with money, they gave a share of the crops to the landlord. A peasant family could not count on the crops doing well every year. Sometimes it was a struggle to earn enough to live on.

Landlords did not usually live on their farms. Instead, they built their homes in local villages and lived there at least part of the year. The farmworkers lived there too. The villages were usually densely settled. One reason peo-

A group of farmworkers relaxes in a village tavern. Most peasants spent their entire lives in small, densely settled villages.

ple crowded together was safety. There was always danger of attack from bandits and others. Therefore, a lord might build a house that was so big that it served as both a home and a kind of fort.

Each village had its own officials to take care of business and other matters. Some of them worked as agents for the local lord, collecting rents and other fees. Not all villagers, though, worked directly for the lord. Among those who usually came from the outside were the village priests, who were appointed by the church.

Both villages and farms used paid workers. Some men were herders, who took care of farm animals, while others carted materials. There were also jobs mining for minerals. Brick making was another way of earning a living. The textile industry was usually located in the city, but both women and men could do spinning and weaving at home. Some people worked at many different jobs, depending on what was needed. They might pick crops in one place, then move on to cut wood somewhere else.

Court Life in the City

At the heart of the city-state was the court of a ruling family. The government of Italy was too weak to protect the whole country, so powerful nobles stepped in to fill this need. The nobles protected the cities and nearby areas. They formed their own armies, wrote laws, created courts, and set up a government. With these actions, they were able to promise a fairly peaceful life for the people under their rule. In return for that promise, the population of a city gave their **loyalty** to the ruling family.

Powerful noble families provided order and protection to the city-states of Italy. They set up governments and created their own armies.

One such ruling family was the Medicis of Florence. They had great wealth, mainly from banking, and their power went well beyond Florence. There were branches of the family both in Italy and in France. Three Medici men served as pope. Two Medici women became queens of France. One—Catherine de Médicis—was the mother of three French kings. She had much power and influence of her own.

Courtiers were the people who were present at a noble's court. Courtiers were expected to be completely loyal to the ruling family and to serve it in different ways. For example, a courtier might act as a go-between for

The Social Order

two powerful families that were always fighting. While at the court, the courtiers were to amuse and entertain the noble's family.

Courtiers were supposed to follow certain rules of conduct. Baldassare Castiglione was born in Mantua and

Catherine de Médicis was the mother of three French kings. The Medici family was very powerful in both Italy and France.

spent time in the courts of Milan and Urbino. Castiglione became famous for writing *The Book of the Courtier,* published in 1528. The book lays out a code of conduct for the perfect courtier. One of the most valued qualities a courtier could have was **grace** in all kinds of situations. As one speaker says, the courtier "in conversing with men and women of every sort . . . [should] possess a certain sweetness and such gracious manners that . . . anyone who speaks with him or even lays eyes on him becomes [forever] fond of him."[3]

Manners were not the only subject covered by helpful books. In 1584 a writer using the name Isabella Cortes wrote a book called *Secrets.* In it, she offered women ideas on how to stay young looking. In a recipe for "Face-Water," she tells the reader to get some white beans. Soak the beans, she writes, in white wine for nine days before pounding them and returning them to the wine. Then the reader must add goat's milk, whole barley, and fresh egg whites. After two weeks, the mixture is ready to use. Says the author, "washing the face with it, it will do a very good job."[4]

The Business of the City

Businesspeople did well during the Renaissance. Some made money from banking, others from manufacturing. They often did business outside their own cities and traded with other countries. Some did so well that they formed a new upper class. However, the ruling families usually tried to keep the political power in their own hands or those of friends.

Businesspeople, such as this banker and his wife, did very well during the Renaissance, often doing business outside their own cities.

There were many small tradesmen, too, who owned stores and sold mainly to local people. Women sometimes got involved in retail trade with their own small shops. A woman might also take over a family-owned business following the death of a husband.

Anyone running a business had to have at least some kind of education. Businesspeople had to keep records and deal with money and tax laws. If they needed extra

The Italian Renaissance

help, there were a number of trained professionals they could hire. These included lawyers, secretaries, and managers. In some parts of Italy, entrance into these fields was open only to the sons of members.

Artisans made and sold their own works. Usually they had workshops in or near their own homes. Though

Artisans of the Renaissance joined organizations known as craft guilds. Each guild had an emblem that represented the crafts its artists made.

they mainly worked on their own, they also formed organizations called craft guilds. The craft guilds made sure that all its members produced high-quality work. They also carefully controlled who entered the guilds.

Other Wage Earners

Two other groups figured in the business of the city. One group was made up of people with few skills who performed various services. They might be servants, laborers, or haulers. Often they were peasants who came in from the country to earn some money in the city.

Finally, there was the clergy. In some of the church's religious **orders**, groups of men or women spent much of their time in prayer. Others did charitable work, such as helping the poor. Priests usually had more contact with everyday life. In the higher ranks of the church were the bishops, who usually came from the ruling families. These connections between the bishops and the nobles were useful because each group could count on the other's help.

People knew what was expected of them within their own class and in dealings between classes. Yet nothing lasted forever, and the people and the rules could change at any time.

CHAPTER THREE

Duties, Dangers, and Delights

Francesco Guicciardini, a Florentine historian, in his collection of sayings called the *Recordi* wrote:

"When I think of the ... number of ways the life of man is subjected to accidents, dangers of [ill health], or chance, or violence, and how many things must [happen together] during a year in order to produce a good harvest, there is nothing [that] amazes me more than seeing an old man or a fertile year.[5]

Life in Renaissance Italy was risky for everyone. Yet there was little time to worry about it. Life was too busy, filled as it was with duties, dangers, and even occasional delights.

Home

At the start of the Renaissance, houses were quite simple and often not very comfortable. People did not have a great many household goods. Those they had were meant to last. Families held on to them, repairing them over and

Duties, Dangers, and Delights

over. They were then handed down to younger members of the family, who used them until they completely wore out.

Those who could afford to do so built solid houses of stone. During the summer, the thick walls kept the house cool. In some rooms, fireplaces supplied heat in the win-

Wealthy Renaissance families built solid stone houses with tiled roofs like this one.

Cooking smells and other odors trapped in the solid stone houses made the air very foul smelling.

ter, though not always enough. The houses were not well lit. Most people used candles, oil lamps, lanterns, or torches hung on the walls, while wealthier families might have **chandeliers**. Even natural light during the day did not help much because windows were small.

The solid houses also trapped the odors of everyday living. Things like burning oil lamps and smoky fireplaces made for foul-smelling air. Cooking smells added to the mix. Not everybody had a kitchen, but those who did tried to place it as far as possible from the rest of the house.

Most homes had no running water, so a town might have a public water source. That meant someone had to take a container to the water and then carry it back.

Women usually did this work. When it came to doing laundry, though, it was easier to carry things to the water. Women would do their wash, then spread the laundry on the grass to dry or hang it on lines outdoors.

There was no piped sewage in Renaissance homes, so there were no indoor toilets. Most people went outdoors to find places set aside for this purpose. These places did not offer much privacy. Wealthier people used chamber pots set inside special chairs in a bedroom or, in some houses, a tiny separate room. Servants then emptied the chamber pot and returned it to its place.

Over time, houses got larger and more comfortable. People were able to improve the comfort of their homes, adding windows, furniture, and **decorative** items. They also hired more servants to look after their new comforts.

Religion and Education

Most Italians were members of the Catholic Church. For the more religious, this meant taking part in the church's rites and rituals. Besides regular services, there were ceremonies that marked all the important moments in life from beginning to end.

Private tutors taught the children of wealthier families and actually lived with them. Some teachers set up little schools in their own homes. Many of them were members of the clergy. In the later years, schools were more organized and usually run by a religious order.

Schooling was not the same for all children. Students who were likely to go on to a university learned Latin so that they could study the classics of ancient Rome. These

The Italian Renaissance

students were mainly males heading for careers in church or government. They learned to be good readers, writers, and speakers, but did not learn such practical skills as how to do everyday mathematics. Only the students who would grow up to work in businesses did that. They studied mainly in Italian, the language of ordinary people. However, all schools tried to pass on rules of good conduct, usually based on religious teachings.

Schooling was not the same for all Renaissance children. Some studied Latin and the classics while others learned mathematics.

Death rides a horse in this Renaissance painting. The plague known as the Black Death killed one-fourth of Europe's population during the Renaissance.

Some students had only a few years of schooling before they went on to work. Often it was church-run schools that offered poorer students their only chance for formal learning. One order of nuns set up schools to give the daughters of these families a religious education. In wealthier families, though, girls received as good an education as their brothers got.

Diseases and Other Ills

Gregorio Dati, a merchant, kept a record of important events in his life. They show how risky life was. Dati was widowed three times. He fathered twenty-six children, eight of whom survived childhood. In one moving entry, he writes about his two-year-old son, "our most beloved, Stagio, our darling and blessed first born. He died of the plague on the morning of Friday, 30 July 1400, in Florence without my seeing him for I was in the country."[6]

An Uncertain Life

The plague that spread across Europe at times was called the Black Death. It wiped out about one-fourth of the population of Europe. In fifteenth-century Florence, two-thirds of the population died. There were many other diseases that had no cures. Childbirth was risky for both mother and child. Infections were hardest on the very young and the old. Poor nutrition and unhealthy conditions in poorer neighborhoods made matters even worse there.

Floods and earthquakes often cost people their homes, if not their lives. Heat waves and frosts might lead to a famine, with many dying from hunger and illness. Sometimes people cleared land that was not good for farming. They cut down forests, drove out the wildlife, destroyed pastures and wetlands, and overcrowded the better locations—all of which led to even more hunger. At such times, the city government would step in and sell grain and seeds, while carefully controlling the price of bread.

Wars and other violence caused many deaths. Sometimes the conflicts were local, with one noble raising an army to take power from a rival. Often the soldiers in those armies were mercenaries, men from other countries hired to fight. When their service ended, the soldiers

Duties, Dangers, and Delights

sometimes became outlaws who took whatever they wanted by force. Since most police were poorly trained and poorly paid, they could not be counted on to control crime.

There was also violence among ordinary citizens. Feuds could break out at any time between groups of young men. Usually the fighting was over an issue of honor. Even a quarrel among neighborhood women might result in violence and soon involve the whole family.

While most Italians were Catholic, there had been a Jewish minority living in Italy since as far back as Roman times. More Jews arrived after fleeing **persecution** in Spain and Portugal. In Italy, how they were treated depended on who was in power. Beginning in the sixteenth

During the Renaissance, frequent wars and smaller conflicts claimed the lives of many people.

century, conditions became **harsher**. Jews were forced to live in separate neighborhoods called ghettos. The overcrowded ghettos had a curfew, at which time the residents were locked inside.

Fashion

Life was not all hardship, though. One of the pleasures, especially for the well-off, was looking as handsome as possible in costumes made just for them. This was true of both men and women. As time went on, though, men and women were told not to stray from what was considered the correct fashion. In some places, there were even written rules on how to dress.

Women especially tried different ways of changing their appearance. They used such tricks as makeup and false hair. Blond was the favorite hair color, and a woman might dye her hair or sit outdoors to let the sun lighten it. Perfumes hid the fact that people did not wash often, and were used freely.

Celebrations

Religious holidays were often times for celebration. Carnival time, before Lent, was the wildest time. There were games, parades, plays, dances, mock fights, and even public punishments. Wearing a mask was popular because people could act freely without anyone knowing who they were. Church officials encouraged the fun, while still keeping things under control, as a notice from Rome in 1601 shows:

> Monday, His Excellency ... got permission from [the pope] for the people of this city to amuse themselves by going around in masks during these last few days

Religious holidays, carnival time, and weddings between members of great families were occasions for huge celebrations like this one in Florence.

of carnival. . . . To encourage the others, the [chief officer of the city] and His Excellency's other children were the first to show themselves . . . with masks.[7]

Weddings between members of two great families also led to huge celebrations that could go on for days. They included parades through the public streets, music, dramas, ballets, races, and wonderful costumes and masks. On such occasions everyone could forget for a time the problems of everyday life—at least until the celebration was over.

CHAPTER FOUR

Artists and Patrons, Thinkers and Doers

During the Renaissance, many great artists produced thousands of beautiful things: sculptures, paintings, **architecture**, poems, speeches, plays, and more. Often those works were commissioned—ordered and paid for—by wealthy patrons. Both artists and patrons looked to ancient Rome and Greece for inspiration.

The Renaissance produced not only great works of art but the model of a person called a Renaissance man or woman, someone admired for having a wide range of skills and interests.

Plato: Inspiration from Greece

When the study of classical Greek became part of the education of many upper- and middle-class Italians, it changed everything. Before, only **scholars** could read the works of Plato. Now many people could study the great thinker in his own language.

Artists and Patrons, Thinkers and Doers

Plato had opened an academy in Greece where students held discussions about how people should behave in their public and private lives. His writings recorded these conversations. The Renaissance patron Lorenzo de' Medici imitated Plato. He set up a Platonic academy in his Florence household. There, great thinkers could meet and discuss Plato's writings. They included many of the people in charge of running the government. In this way,

Lorenzo de' Médici (seated, center) and members of his family discuss the works of the ancient Greek thinker Plato at Lorenzo's Platonic academy in Florence.

The Italian Renaissance

Plato's ideas had an effect on the way the city-states of Italy were run.

Cicero: Inspiration from Rome

Cicero was also concerned with how people behaved. In fact, he studied Plato's work and took some of his ideas from it. Cicero was a great speaker and writer. He believed in having a republic, a form of government in which citizens choose their leaders. There were times in Italy when some city-states actually had a republic. Usually, though,

Cicero (at desk, left) is hard at work in this Renaissance painting.

strong leaders like the Medicis would take over, and the dream of a republic remained just that.

Cicero improved Latin so much that it outlasted ancient Rome. For hundreds of years, people all over the world studied his writings and used Latin in their own work. It was Cicero's Latin that most Renaissance teachers held up as the perfect model for their students.

Petrarch: Improving on the Past

Francesco Petrarca, or Petrarch, was born in 1304. He recognized the genius of Cicero, whose work he read in the original Latin. Though he read Plato and other Greeks only in translation, Petrarch became a well-known scholar of ancient cultures. It was Petrarch, more than any other person, who rediscovered these and other great classical writers. He was also famous for his own poetry. Petrarch's poetry echoed great Latin and Greek literature but also went beyond it. Later, many great writers in Europe would look to Petrarch's work for their inspiration.

Isabella d'Este: In Search of Beauty

When patrons commissioned a work of art from a great artist, they were often thinking of the honor that would attach to their names because of it. However, some patrons collected great art simply because they wished to be surrounded by beauty. Isabella d'Este was a patron of the arts, and she filled her homes with the sights and sounds of great art. She herself was a gifted musician. When called upon, she also showed how well she could govern and handle dealings with other leaders.

The Italian Renaissance

Isabella d'Este was a patron of the arts. She commissioned works from great Renaissance artists.

Sometimes patrons were very exact about what they wanted from an artist. In a letter to Leonardo da Vinci, Isabella d'Este spelled out exactly what she wanted in a painting from him. However, artists need freedom to create the images in their minds, which may not be what their patrons have ordered. Of course, an artist could always turn down a commission from a patron. Sometimes the artist would just take so long completing a commission that the patron would finally give up. Then they might either take whatever the artist was willing to paint or commission another artist.

That is what happened with Isabella and Leonardo. On May 14, 1504, she wrote from Mantua:

> If you will consent to [satisfy] this our great desire [to have a work from your hand], remember that apart from the payment, which you shall fix yourself, we shall remain so deeply [grateful] to you that our sole desire will be to do what you wish, and from this time forth we are ready to do your service and pleasure.[8]

Artist Leonardo da Vinci was also an expert in math, engineering, and science.

Leonardo da Vinci: Observer of Nature

When Isabella d'Este first tried to contact Leonardo through a friend, that man told her that Leonardo was tired of painting and was busy studying geometry. Leonardo not only painted but was also expert in math, engineering, and science. He was interested in knowing how everything worked, and he felt he could learn much by studying nature. He especially enjoyed watching and drawing birds in flight.

Unlike other artists, Leonardo did not look to the past for inspiration. He felt that repeating what others had done would not be good for art. Art should be original. Nor was he the only one who felt that too much attention was being paid to the past. To be like the Romans, Francesco Guicciardini wrote in the *Ricordi*, "one would have to have a city with conditions exactly like theirs and then to govern it according to their example."[9]

Leonardo was more interested in the future. His interest in flight led him to design ways humans might fly too. He sketched ideas for flying machines—including helicopters—and even designed a parachute. He did all of this hundreds of years before these things were actually invented.

Michelangelo: Genius in Many Forms

Michelangelo Buonarroti was born in 1475 to a family of Florentines. As with other Renaissance men, he was inspired by the past but talented enough to go beyond it. His early work caught the eye of Lorenzo de' Medici, the powerful ruler of Florence at the time. Sometimes a wealthy patron invited an artist to live in his or her palace. That is what happened with Michelangelo. When the Medicis lost power, though, he was able to travel. In Rome, Michelangelo's sculpture was so powerful and beautiful that he soon became one of the best-known artists in Italy.

Michelangelo once complained in a letter, "I cannot live under pressures from patrons, let alone paint."[10]

Da Vinci's *Mona Lisa* is one of the most famous works of art from the Renaissance.

The Italian Renaissance

By pressures, he meant impatient patrons who wanted the artists to complete the work right away and do it just their way. Michelangelo, however, usually got his own way because he was Michelangelo. He would not agree to a contract that spelled out exactly what he was to do.

Michelangelo not only created great sculptures but painted and tried architecture as well. He also spent some time writing poetry, especially when he was older.

Michelangelo is one of the Renaissance's best-known artists.

Michelangelo painted the *Creation of Adam* and other scenes from the Bible on the ceiling of the Sistine Chapel in Rome.

All Good Things

The Renaissance took place in a harsh world full of wars, plagues, and cruelty. Still, it produced some of the most talented men and women of that or any other time. Though the Italian Renaissance itself ended in Italy about 1600, its effects were felt everywhere and for many years. Styles and tastes have changed over the years, but the great literature, paintings, architecture, and sculpture of the Italian Renaissance are still recognized as masterpieces.

Notes

Chapter One: The Birth of the Renaissance

1. Quoted in Julia Conaway Bondanella and Mark Musa, eds., *The Italian Renaissance Reader.* New York: Meridian, 1987, p. 308.
2. Quoted in Leon Battista Alberti, *The Family in Renaissance Florence,* (Book Three), trans. Renée Neu Watkins. Illinois: Waveland Press, 1994, p. 13.

Chapter Two: The Social Order

3. Quoted in Bondanella and Musa, *The Italian Renaissance Reader,* p. 209.
4. Quoted in Elizabeth S. Cohen and Thomas V. Cohen, *Daily Life in Renaissance Italy.* Connecticut: Greenwood Press, 2001, p. 236.

Chapter Three: Duties, Dangers, and Delights

5. Quoted in Bondanella and Musa, *The Italian Renaissance Reader,* p. 301.
6. Quoted in Cohen and Cohen, *Daily Life in Renaissance Italy,* p. 183.
7. Quoted in Archivio di Stato di Firenze, Mediceo del Principato 4028, c. 23. The Medici Archive Project. www.medici.org/news/dom/dom042001.html.

Chapter Four: Artists and Patrons, Thinkers and Doers

8. Quoted in Julia Cartwright, *Isabella D'Este: Marchioness of Mantua, 1474–1539: A Study of the Renaissance,* vol.

1. 1915. Reprint, Hawaii: University Press of the Pacific, 2002, pp. 324–25.
9. Quoted in Bondanella and Musa, *The Italian Renaissance Reader,* pp. 300–301.
10. Quoted in Peter Burke, *The Italian Renaissance: Culture and Society in Italy,* 2nd ed. New Jersey: Princeton University Press, 1999, p. 89.

Glossary

architecture: The art of building.

artisan: A worker who is skilled in a particular trade, such as carpentry, baking, or weaving.

chandelier: A lighting fixture hung from the ceiling and holding many lights.

decorative: Pleasing to the eye.

dialect: A language spoken by a group of people and differing somewhat from the original language and other forms of that language.

endure: Put up with; suffer through.

grace: A pleasing quality; charm; style.

harsh: Difficult; cruel.

loyalty: The feeling of owing allegiance to a country, person, or organization.

order: A religious organization, such as a group of monks or nuns.

persecution: The act of treating badly; harming.

scholar: One who has great knowledge.

scholarly: Showing great knowledge.

scholarship: The quality of learning.

thriving: Succeeding; doing well.

For Further Exploration

Books

Robert Byrd, *Leonardo: Beautiful Dreamer.* New York: Dutton, 2003. Celebrates the accomplishments of one of the world's greatest geniuses. Vividly illustrated by the author.

Giovanni Caselli, *The Renaissance and the New World.* New York: Peter Bedrick, 1998. Part of the History of Everyday Things series, this book takes readers on a world tour from 1400 to 1780. Colorful illustrations include cutaway views of palaces.

Alison Cole, *Eyewitness: Renaissance.* New York: Dorling Kindersley, 2000. This art history book has many reproductions of works by Renaissance artists and historical information with many little-known facts.

Andrew Langley, *Eyewitness: Leonardo and His Times.* New York: Dorling Kindersley, 2001. Basic information about the social forces that moved societies from the medieval era to the Renaissance. Illustrations and reproductions of period artwork, plus cutaways of buildings.

Jacqueline Morley et al., *A Renaissance Town.* New York: Peter Bedrick, 2001. Explores how people lived and worked and how their towns were built.

Websites

The Art Guide of Florence (www.mega.it/eng/egui/hogui.htm). Students can explore the monuments, historic periods, artists, and artworks of Florence.

45

Italian Renaissance Architecture (http://rubens.anu.edu.au/htdocs/surveys/italren/renarch). Students are a click or two away from viewing the work of artists mentioned in the text, such as Leon Battista Alberti and Michelangelo.

Italian Renaissance Clothing (www.twingroves.district96.k12.il.us/Renaissance/Town/Clothing/ClothingItalian.html). The text gives details on fabrics and costumes and links to images of actual clothing and hairstyles.

Italian Renaissance Gardens (www.arts.monash.edu.au/visual_culture/projects/diva/italian.html). Landscaping was yet another form of Renaissance art, and students can explore these beautiful sites in Italy.

Tour: Italian Renaissance Ceramics (www.nga.gov/collection/gallery/itacer/itacer-main1.html). The National Gallery of the United States offers a virtual tour of the output of some of the great craftsmen of Italy.

WebMuseum, Paris (www.ibiblio.org/wm/paint/tl/it-ren). A virtual museum that allows students to learn more about Renaissance art and gives them the opportunity to view the works of the great artists.

Index

Alberti, Leon Battista, 7–8
appearance, 12, 18, 30
artisans, 20–21

banking, 8
Black Death, 28
Book of the Courtier, The (Castiglione), 18
Book of the Family (Alberti), 7–8
businesspeople, 18–19

carnival time, 30–31
Castiglione, Baldassare, 17–18
Catholic Church, 21, 25–27, 29
Cellini, Benvenuto, 7, 11
childbirth, 28
Cicero, 34–35
city-states, 4–5
classics, of ancient Greek and Rome
    discovery and translation of, 7–8
    study of, 25
clergy, 21
Cortes, Isabella, 18
courtiers, 16–18
craft guilds, 21

Dati, Gregorio, 27–28
death, 27–28
d'Este, Isabella, 35–37
diseases, 27–28

earthquakes, 28

economy, of Florence, 8
education, 25–27

farms, 12–15
fashions, 30
floods, 28
Florence (Italy), 4, 7, 8, 11

government, 15, 28
Greco-Roman civilization
    study of classics from, 25
    traces of, 5, 7
Guicciardini, Francesco, 22
guilds, 21

holidays, religious, 30–31
Holy Roman Empire, 5
homes, 22–25

Italian Renaissance
    birth of, 4, 8, 11
    end of, 41

Judaism, 29–30

laborers, 21
landlords, 12–15
languages, 4–5, 7, 25–26, 35
Latin, 5, 7, 25–26, 35
Leonardo da Vinci, 36–38

Medici, Lorenzo de', 33, 38
Medici family, 16
mercenaries, 28–29
Michelangelo Buonarroti, 38, 40

47

natural disasters, 28
nobles, 12–15, 31
    see also patrons

patrons, pressure from, 38, 40
peasants, 13–15, 21
perfumes, 30
Petrarch, Francesco Petrarca, 35
plague, 28
Plato, 32–34
priests, 21
printing press, 8
professionals, 20

Recordi (Guicciardini), 22
Roman Empire, 6, 8
ruins, 7
ruling families, 15–17, 18

Secrets (Cortes), 18
society, place in, 12

textiles, 8
tradesmen, 19
Tuscany (Italy), 8

villages, 14–15

wars, 28–29
weddings, 31
women
    appearance of, 18, 30
    in business, 19
    childbirth and, 28
    education of, 27
    housework done by, 24–25
    place in society of, 12

APR 0 7 2004
MAY 2 8 2004
J 945.05